FIFTY
ROCHDALE
RECORDS

ROCHDALE OBSERVER FIFTY ROCHDALE RECORDS

ROCHDALE METROPOLITAN BOROUGH COUNCIL

Richard Catlow and John Cole

Breedon Books
Publishing Company
Derby

First published in Great Britain by
The Breedon Books Publishing Company Limited
Breedon House, 44 Friar Gate, Derby, DE1 1DA.
1998

Dedicated to our wives, Helen and Sue

ISBN 1 85983 133 8

Printed and bound by Butler & Tanner Ltd., Selwood Printing Works,
Caxton Road, Frome, Somerset.

Colour separations by Freelance Repro, Leicester.

Jackets printed by Lawrence-Allen, Avon.

CONTENTS

INTRODUCTION

IT STARTED as an idle query over lunch. It continued – via the columns of the *Rochdale Observer* – getting hundreds of people talking, older folk remembering, younger ones researching and finished by becoming a project which will provide a centrepiece of Rochdale's Millennium celebrations.

It was a simple question: "Has Rochdale produced more famous people and significant events than any other town its size?"

The attempt to discover the answer has produced this book and very good grounds for saying that the answer is "Yes".

In fact our attempt to find *50 Rochdale Records* produced rather more than that and we've had to double up on some of them. Even so, we are sure that there will be more we have failed to write about.

The records are pesented in chronological order, from earliest times to the present with, we're sure, many more to come.

From the book came the idea of an exhibition for the town's eagerly-awaited Arts and Heritage Centre, from that sprung the plan to create a travelling exhibition to celebrate Millennium Year

involving people and communities throughout the Borough.

50 Rochdale Records began as fun and has been full of surprises and enjoyment along the way. But, in an unexpected way, it has also become a broad-ranging history of Rochdale in a way that has never been done before.

We hope you will get as much pleasure from it as we have.

Richard Catlow
John Cole

ACKNOWLEDGEMENTS

Photographs courtesy of the Rochdale Observer archives and Rochdale Local Studies Library.

Thanks to: Andy Wiggars for proof-reading during the World Cup; Trevor Hoyle for permission to quote from his novel *Rule of the Night*; Gracie Fields expert Debbie Walker for Gracie information; local historian Ron Stables for Roger Fenton material; Mr H.Swain for his Moss Row stories; Nan Jackson for the information on Belfield Community School; Pam Godman for sharing her knowledge of the Blackstone Edge Road; and to the people of Rochdale, past and present, without whom there would be no Rochdale Records.

50 ROCHDALE RECORDS

1

THE OLDEST SCORPION IN LANCASHIRE (and the finest arthropod fossil find)

Workmen with fossil trees found at Sparth Bottom in September, 1894.

BURIED in Rochdale is evidence of life on earth 240 million years ago!

In the 1890s and early 1900s the scientific community was shaken by a series of fossil discoveries at Sparth Bottoms. The area had long been famous for the fossilised plants which turned up regularly in the Coal Measures when, in September 1894, workmen unearthed a whole tree!

Six years later, the foreman at the local brickworks "broke open an almost spherical nodule of clay ironstone which contained a beautiful fossil crustacean."

Various other crab-like forms were discovered and over the next few years a stream of learned articles appeared in the

specialist journals.

Then, in 1903, an entirely new species of scorpion was found, reverently named "Eoscorpius Sparthensis" in recognition of the area of its discovery.

The collection is still referred to as "a unique arthropod fauna find" giving Sparth "a hugely prominent place in the Palaentological world" – and its very own scorpion!

BRITAIN'S MOST MYSTERIOUS ROAD

EVER since people have been interested in the origin of such things – and that's more than two centuries now – historians have argued over whether the remarkable stone road over Blackstone Edge was built by the Romans.

Countless people, many of them experts, have divided over this question and still, amazingly, there is no firm consensus whether the stone setted road with its striking central groove is or is not a legacy of the Roman occupation.

One thing only unites the experts and that is that the road, whether Roman or mediaeval in date, is a structure almost without comparison in Britain. If Roman it is the best preserved section of ancient highway in Britain. If

An atmospheric picture looking down the Roman Road towards Littleborough and clearly showing the central groove – was it used for braking or drainage?

mediaeval it is in a different league to any other route and if an early turnpike is quite different in structure to any other.

The main argument against Roman origins is the fact that no fortresses or other military structures are found along its route. An undoubted Roman highway runs just a few miles south of the route and visitors to Castleshaw can see a very obvious Roman fort to this day.

But the Blackstone Edge road is so solid and well-engineered that it represents a standard of highway making that was never equalled between the fall of Rome and the mid-18th century.

Local historian Pam Godman has recently discovered what is almost certainly a continuation of the road nearer to Littleborough

Running from Lane Head over the hills to Rossendale is the Rooley Moor Road, sometimes known as the "Cotton Famine Road".

The road earned its nickname because it was re-surfaced with stone setts as a job creation scheme during the Cotton Famine brought on by the American Civil War. Although rough enough in sections to deter motor vehicles, long stretches of fine setts remain.

Rising to almost 1,500ft, does it make this the highest "cobbled street" around?

The stone setts of the Rooley Moor Road heading upwards to distant Rossendale.

3

The old Rochdale Market in Lord Street about 1910.

AMONGST THE FIRST MARKETS IN LANCASHIRE

THE recorded or written history of Rochdale begins in 1086 with the Domesday Survey of William the Conqueror. Rochdale, then written Recedham, was held by a landowner, or thane, called Gamel. As a Saxon thane held not only land but also a church, it is probable that Rochdale's Parish Church existed then.

Indeed, as the church is dedicated to St Chad, who was

The entrance to the market today.

The old Top Market on a busy Saturday afternoon in 1960.

Bishop of Lichfield in the seventh century, it could be even older.

The Parish and Manor of Rochdale covered the same territory, a huge, sprawling tract of waste and moorland from Ashworth in the west to Bacup and Saddleworth in the north and east. The De Lacy family, Lords of Clitheroe and Pontefract, acquired the Rochdale Manor in the twelfth century and in 1251 Edmund de Lacy was granted the right from the King to hold a weekly Wednesday market at Rochdale and an annual fair on 27, 28 and 29 October.

Rochdale's was amongst the very first market charters to be granted in Lancashire and for centuries the importance of the town was not as a place of manufacture but as a market centre for trade and commerce where food and livestock, and most importantly wool and cloth, were bought and sold.

Originally situated near the present Church Lane, the market was transferred to the bottom of Yorkshire Street in the mid-16th century. Those travelling through the town were warned to stay away on market days – or face a three-hour delay fighting past stall holders, pedlars, hawkers and thousands of townsfolk and visitors. Literally scores of inns and taverns became centres of trade where the deals were struck which sent Rochdale woollens, kerseys and flannels throughout Europe, Asia and the New World, paving the way for the textile boom that fuelled the Industrial Revolution.

MOST CHURCHES AND CHAPELS (and the first Sunday School in the North)

BAPTISTS, Congregationalists, Presbyterians, Unitarians, Primitive Methodists, the United Methodist Free Church, the Church of England, the Roman Catholic Church, the Society of Friends, Swedenborgians, Cookites, the Countess of Huntingdon's Connexion: historian G.D.H. Cole doubted "if any town of Rochdale's size was equally prolific in religious controversy and foundations".

"New churches and chapels", he noted, "were continually being formed". The phenomenon continues to this day with the town supporting over 25 mosques. In the 19th century all this religious activity had serious political overtones. If you were a regular worshipper at St Chad's Parish Church, the chances were you had Tory sympathies; if you were a member of the Baillie Street United Methodist Free Church you were probably a reforming Liberal and if you attended the Clover Street Unitarian or Smith Street Primitive Methodist Chapels you were an out-and-out radical.

All of these churches and chapels with their political affiliations sought to capture the hearts and minds of children and young people via their Sunday Schools and it is probable that Rochdale had the earliest Sunday School in the North.

Robert Raikes established the first ever Sunday School in Gloucester in 1780 and was quickly engaged in correspondence with Richard Townley of Rochdale. Townley in turn approached James Hamilton, a local tinmaker who established a Sunday School in White Beaver Yard Rochdale early in 1783. The idea spread like wildfire with some schools merely attempting to channel working class children's energies into

The oldest church in Rochdale, the parish church of St Chad.

The town's newest place of worship, the mosque on Castlemere Street, showing members with Abdul Hameed Waraich (Pakistan High Commissioner) and MP Lorna Fitzsimons as it neared completion.

non-threatening, improving activities whilst many others actually provided the only instructions in the "three R's" that the sons and daughters of the poor ever received.

Both objectives met with limited success. From the 1840s, instruction in reading and writing was phased out. As for the channelling of youthful energies, the following passage from Robert Standring's reminiscence of Lanehead Sunday School in the 1820s would indicate that this was an uphill struggle:

I have once seen the Holy Book thrown furiously to the ground by a boy who was being punished. At another time a boy was being punished for one little thing or another when his sufferings enraged him so much that he drew a large clasp knife and threatened to stab any teacher who would threaten him again.

Clearly classroom violence is no modern phenomenon.

The Victorian age was a time of great religious enthusiasm, especially among Nonconformist churches. Pictured here, in Wardle Square, is the Wesleyan Home Mission caravan in 1882.

FLANNEL CAPITAL OF BRITAIN

THE development of Rochdale's textile industry was unique in Lancashire. The early local woollen industry was based upon the smallholders and farmer-weavers whose cottages were scattered over the 11 square miles of bleak moorland which constituted the Parish of Rochdale.

In the late 16th century, those areas specialising in linen production – particularly Oldham, Bolton and Blackburn – began experimenting with a cloth which combined a linen warp (the vertical thread) with a cotton weft (the horizontal thread) to produce fustian.

At roughly the same time in traditional woollen areas, including (because of its proximity to wool-producing Yorkshire) Rochdale, worsted was combined with wool to produce a cheap, light cloth known as bays.

Fustian spread rapidly throughout Lancashire until, by the end of the first half of the 17th century, the woollen industry was confined to the eastern fringe of the county with Rochdale as its most important centre.

The staple manufacture of the Rochdale area became a branch of the woollen trade consisting chiefly of baizes, kerseys, coatings, cloths and flannels.

Coarse flannel, designed to offer the least possible irritation to the skin, consisted of Irish worsted warps and woollen wefts and had previously been manufactured in Wales – particularly in the Newport, Pontypool and Abergavenny areas.

In the mid-18th century, these products succumbed to the confusingly-named "real Welch flannel" from Rochdale.

Thus, while the fustian producing areas (Oldham, Bolton etc) became by natural transition the original cotton towns, Rochdale developed into the national centre of coarse or plain-weave flannel.

Flannel weaving at Kelsall and Kemp around 1935.

6

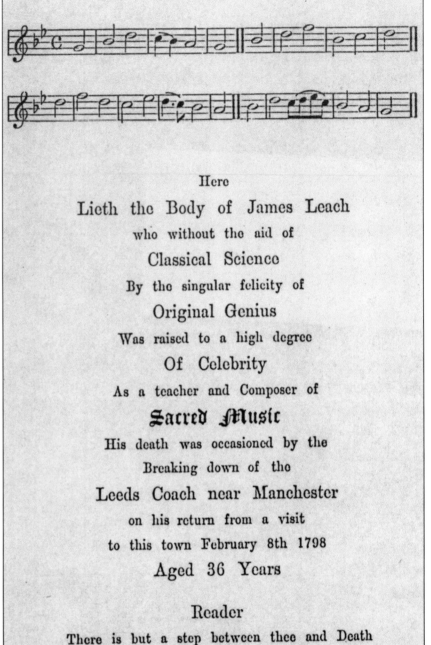

Here
Lieth the Body of James Leach
who without the aid of
Classical Science
By the singular felicity of
Original Genius
Was raised to a high degree
Of Celebrity
As a teacher and Composer of
𝔖𝔞𝔠𝔯𝔢𝔡 𝔐𝔲𝔰𝔦𝔠
His death was occasioned by the
Breaking down of the
Leeds Coach near Manchester
on his return from a visit
to this town February 8th 1798
Aged 36 Years

Reader
There is but a step between thee and Death

A copy of the inscription on the gravestone of James Leach.

JAMES LEACH: LANCASHIRE'S FOREMOST HYMN WRITER

JAMES Leach was widely regarded in the last century as *THE* Lancashire composer. Perhaps not surprisingly, in view of the village's current reputation for music making, James Leach was born, in 1762, in Wardle.

Largely self-taught musically, with little or no general education, Leach proved a naturally gifted musician. He became a renowned concerto-tenor singer, pianist and choir-master and in 1789 published his first volume of sacred music.

A second volume followed in 1797 and contained many hymns which were to become standards for Methodist congregations in Britain and America.

On 8 February 1798, Leach was travelling to Manchester by coach when, just outside Blackley, the speeding vehicle lost a wheel and overturned. Leach, who was thrown from the coach, died instantly.

His gravestone inscription from the Union Street Wesleyan Chapel is reproduced below. It began with his tune "Egypt" and ended with a chilling prediction. The stone's present whereabouts are unknown but, as the site of the graveyard is under the busy St Mary's Gate dual carriageway, there certainly is, as the inscription warns, "but a step between thee and death."

The remarkable picture of Rochdale Races that hangs in the golf club. As you can see, the racing was only a small part of entertainment.

ROCHDALE RACES – THE OLDEST IN LANCASHIRE

THE first Grand National took place in 1839. The Rochdale Races, claimed to be the earliest in Lancashire, began over 100 years earlier in Saddleworth. In 1723, when the first race meeting was organised, Saddleworth formed part of the Ancient Parish of Rochdale – and was also within the boundaries of Rochdale Manor. So in October of that year the wealthy merchants and landowners of Rochdale gathered on the open moors for a day's sport. Having obviously enjoyed this outing, they repeated it the following year.

By the 1770s, however, the races had transferred to Hunger Hill, Rooley Moor and then to Whittaker Moss, south of Edenfield Road. The collapse of the grandstand, resulting in the death of a Mary Sharples of

Bamford, caused the races to be moved once again - this time to Bagslate Common, the site of the present golf course.

The revived races at Bagslate proved hugely popular. Jugglers, tinkers, hawkers, toffee makers, pedlars, pickpockets and punters thronged to the annual meeting. The Lord of the Manor sponsored the richest prize – the Manor Plate – in 1828 worth a respectable £50 and the racing card was supplemented by numerous other activities including cockfighting, footraces, boxing matches, donkey derbies - and drinking.

It was a grand day out and the new reforming middle

classes hated it! They argued, that the Lord of the Manor and his entourage were setting a poor example.

Undeterred, in 1845, they erected a grandstand on Bagslate Common. By some oversight, however, they neglected to pay for it. When, therefore, in 1850, a horse belonging to James Pilling of Bridgefield won two races and the Committee failed to raise the prize money, the indignant Mr Pilling simply claimed the grandstand.

The resulting confusion effectively killed off the Bagslate Races but a fabulous record survives in the form of a painting executed in 1850 in household paint directly on to wood which is today in the possession of Rochdale Golf Club.

The races live on in the name of the Turf Tavern, on Edenfield Road.

8

THE FATHER OF LANCASHIRE DIALECT WRITING

IT'S hard to believe now when relatively little is published and much of that twee rather than authentic, that books and poems in the Lancashire Dialect were once hugely popular and sold in countless thousands; not only in Lancashire but much further afield.

It's the only English dialect with which this happened and for that we can thank an 18th century schoolmaster from Milnrow whose pen name is still famous to this day; not least on Lancashire pub signs.

Tim Bobbin's fame stems from his book *A View of the Lancashire Dialect*, published in 1746, which takes the form of a comic dialogue between two Lancashire worthies: Thomas and Mary.

The humour of a simple soul let loose in a complex world made it a best-seller, but to John Collier (as Tim Bobbin was properly called) it was also a groundbreaking work of much scholarship and research, accompanied by a glossary of Lancashire words and phrases he had recorded over the years.

Tim Bobbin was far more than a village humourist. Of humble origins he may have been, but he was also very much the well-rounded 18th-century man of letters.

A particular talent – and one that earned almost as much fame as his writing – was as an engraver. His funny and biting satire on corrupt clergy and state officials, *Human Passions Delineated,* was massively popular and earned him the sobriquet "the Lancashire Hogarth".

Born in 1708 in Urmston, near Manchester, Tim Bobbin was apprenticed to a weaver, but gave this up to become a travelling teacher; travelling mainly in the areas around

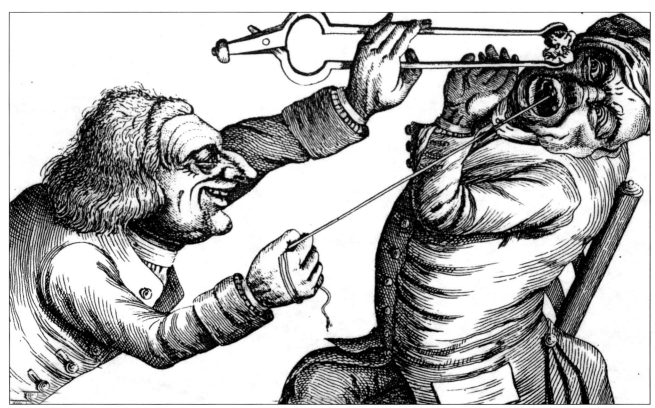

Two of Tim Bobbin's satirical engravings, showing why he earned the title *The Lancashire Hogarth.*

Rochdale, Oldham and Bury.

In 1726 he became assistant schoolmaster at Milnrow, where he was to remain for virtually the rest of his life.

He married, aged 36, and he and his wife produced nine children. When Tim died, in 1786, he was buried alongside his wife in the graveyard of St Chad's, the Parish Church of Rochdale where his tomb can be seen to this day. The grave bears the lines from one of his most famous verses beginning: "Here lies Tom and with him Mary, Cheek by jowl they never vary"; thus identifying Tim and his wife with his most celebrated characters.

9

PUREST FORM OF LANCASHIRE DIALECT

DESPITE, or perhaps because, of its proximity to Yorkshire, Rochdale's form of Lancashire dialect was considered the purest.

Certainly as far as the art of transcribing dialect to the printed page was concerned, the local practitioners were the original and best.

John Collier, or "Tim Bobbin", Milnrow school-teacher, cartoonist, eccentric and historian, who wrote his glossary of Lancashire dialect in 1745, is generally regarded as the pioneer; Rochdale's Edwin Waugh (1817-1890) was the Poet Laureate.

Sentimental, often; nostalgic, certainly; dialect poetry sought to celebrate and perpetuate the traditions of a pre-industrial world revolving around family and friendship.

Here's a taster by Rochdale's John Trafford Clegg (1857-1895) celebrating the Rochdale (Rachda) Wakes holiday and the fair on the Holme Cattle Market opposite the Town Hall.

Rachda Wakes - John Trafford Clegg

*Come, Betty, lass, it's Rachda
    Wakes;
Let's ramble into th' teawn,
An' fee o' 'brandy-snaps an' cakes,
Wi pop to west 'em deawn.
There's bobby-horses, dry lond
    sails,
Pikin folk up i'crops,
Quack doctors wi o maksi tales,
An' likeness-takkin' shops
    (photograph shops)
There's shootin-galleries so long
'At hobry th'end con see;
Blowing machines for wynt-pipes
    stroung,
An swing-boats flying hee.
There's cowd ice-cream, thin
    lemonade,
Black pudding boilt an' fried
Wot pieghs, ham sangwidges, cake
    brade, (hot pies) an' lots of
    things beside.
But that's o nowt to th'penny
    shows
We'll goo to them o reaund;
An' there's a circus too, tha knows,
On th' cattle-market greaund.
Th' fat women's comn again,
    an'th'pig,
Th' wild-beast show, wi'th' owd
    smell;
An' Buckskin Billy playing tig
Wi Indians o on th' yell (All
    whopping)
Aw'll buy thee sich a fairin" lass,
As th's ne'er had afore;
An' tha'll be th'prattiest theere, bi
    th'mass,
Though there'll be money a score.
An' when it o'er aw'll link thee
    wom (take you home)
Through qiest fielt an 'lone,
An' afore another Wakes con come
Wi cortin we'll ha'done.*

10

WHAT A LOCK WE'VE GOT!

THE building of the Rochdale Canal in 1794 also gave us a record: the North's highest concentration of canal locks. The Rochdale Canal rises from 162ft above sea level in Manchester to 600ft at Summit; by canal standards an enormous climb, then falls 319ft to Sowerby Bridge. To cross the Pennines in this way took the enormous number of 92 locks (not to mention eight aqueducts and a tunnel).

The biggest concentration of locks is around Littleborough.

ENGLAND'S INLAND SEASIDE RESORT

THE 18th century saw burgeoning industry in the towns of east Lancashire and the West Riding of Yorkshire so it was natural that, even though the Pennines lay between them, efforts would be made to link them by canal.

The Rochdale Canal, running from Manchester to Sowerby Bridge, was one of three trans-Pennine canals. Begun in 1794 and finished a decade later, it suffered the disadvantage of all canals in hilly areas; that of needing vast quantities of water to keep its upper levels filled because of the locks emptying it away on either side. Part of the answer to this problem was the building of a giant reservoir at Hollingworth Lake. The lake has a shore line of two miles, 372 yards and an average depth of 30ft. A steam engine pumped water 45 feet higher up the hillside into a channel which conducted the water to where it was needed most at Summit. From an early date it was clear that the lake was no ordinary reservoir but a creation of much wider interest, attracting considerable numbers of visitors who would walk its shores.

The Canal Company leased the use of the lake, separate from the water rights, to two local men to develop it as a tourist attraction. It became known as the "Weighvers' Seaport"; in effect the country's only inland seaside resort.

Hotels, refreshments rooms, pleasure gardens and activities such as fishing, rowing and sailing brought people by the thousand. The railway companies advertised excursions to the lake which by now had become Rochdale's answer to Blackpool.

The first of a series of famous regattas was held in 1856 and the rowing club was good enough to enter a team at Henley.

The original local pubs were joined by grander edifices, such as the Beach Hotel and the splendid Lake Hotel and Gardens.

The Beach offered gaslit dancing for up to 2,000 people while the Lake was reached by a steamer ferry which could be called by telegraph using a cable on the bed of the lake. Passengers landed at a special floating landing stage.

The Lake was famous for its gardens which catered for picnics and wedding breakfasts. In August, 1866, 6,000 miners held a conference here!

Other establishments and amusements sprang up around the shores, including the famous Bobby Horses, a steam-powered ride.

The Lake has always exerted a magnetic attraction for young people. In the 1930s and 1940s it was one of the local "chicken runs". Young men and women would parade around the Lakeside hoping to "trap" with a member of the opposite sex.

In the 1950s Teddy Boys gathered there; in the sixties it was the mods and rockers. In 1975 local author Trevor Hoyle published his Rochdale-set documentary novel "Rule of the Night". The book follows the adventure and misadventures of a group of teenagers as they try to make sense of the bleak post-industrial world of the mid-1970s.

In the following extract they visit Hollingworth Lake – proposing a couple of Rochdale Records of their own:

On the Rakewood Viaduct the motorway traffic buzzed like a quiet yet angry swarm of bees

"It's the highest motorway bridge in England', Shortarse said.

"The longest', Arthur said

*"The **** highest," Shortarse said.*

Across the smooth, dead surface of the Lake the lights of the Lakeside Restaurant shone hard and bright in the still air. A

A bustling scene outside the Lake Hotel, Hollingworth Lake, in around 1920.

car's headlights flashed briefly over the water and turned a semi-circle to follow the dust road which wound along the edge of the Lake for half a mile till it changed into tarmacadam. There was nothing moving on the Lake, not a yacht, not a buoy, not a fish.

"It's the coldest water in England this", said Shortarse.

Arthur scoffed. "It is!" Shortarse said, his voice an octave higher.

"You'll be telling us next there's a village underneath it," Kenny said, which was the local rumour handed down over several generations.

"There bloody is," Shortarse said.

"And you can hear the church bells ringing under the water."

"You can," Shortarse said.

Well, there was a farm there in 1799 but unfortunately no church or village.

The coldest water story was probably created to deter swimmers but young Shortarse was right about one thing – the Rakewood Viaduct is the highest motorway bridge in England.

With easier travel and better wages the attractions of the lake lost out to other destinations. Even today, though, the lake gets large numbers of visitors at weekends and Good Friday is still a lively occasion.

The countryside centre is a new attraction and its excellent interpretive displays of local life and landscapes brings in visitors from far and wide.

50 ROCHDALE RECORDS

12

THE WORLD'S MOST ROMANTIC LORD OF THE MANOR

IT MAY be a cliché, but George Gordon, 6th Baron Byron of Rochdale, was the world's first media superstar. Flamboyant, intense, athletic and broodingly handsome, Byron blazed like a comet through Georgian Society.

Born in London in 1788, Byron succeeded his uncle to become Lord of the Manor of Rochdale in 1808.

As befits a dashing romantic poet, Byron was practically broke when he came to Hopwood Hall, Middleton in 1811 to prove his title to the family estate and sell it (a process which was to prove so complicated that it took over 10 years to complete).

True to form, whilst at Hopwood, Byron "made himself very acceptable to the ladies who took care to let him know they regarded him as a Lion".

The Lion did, however, find time to work in Hopwood's library on the final draft of his most famous poem "Childe Harolde".

This was to be Byron's only visit to the area. Scandal linking him with his own sister eventually forced him to leave the country. He ended his swashbuckling life in 1824 fighting for the cause of Greek independence – a cause to which he donated the £34,000 he finally obtained from the sale of Rochdale Manor.

Lord Byron, Rochdale's romantic baron.

ONLY TOWN IN BRITAIN WITH TWO CIRCULAR BOUNDARIES

Rochdale was a Parish dating back at least to the appointment of its first vicar in 1194, if not before. Rochdale, then known as Recedham, was also the town at the centre of the Parish.

Because of the huge area covered by both the Parish and the Manor of Rochdale (including Bacup, Saddleworth and part of Todmorden), the administrative unit was divided into four townships. These were Spotland (including Whitworth, Brandwood and Bacup), Castleton (including the present Castleton), Butterworth (including Milnrow) and Hundersfield (including Wardle, Littleborough, Todmorden and Saddleworth).

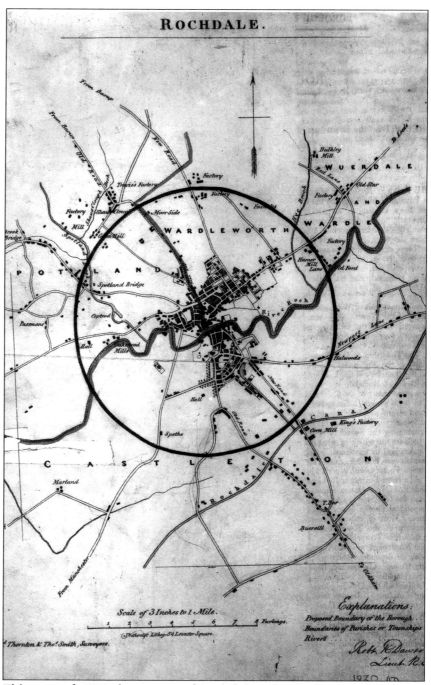

This map of 1832 shows one of Rochdale's circular boundaries.

The four townships converged in the centre of the town of Rochdale which, as a result, had no co-ordinated local administration. In 1825, the local Police Act established a rudimentary form of local government, including the creation of beadles and watchmen. In order to define a boundary, a centre point was identified "very near to the south east corner of an archway or road leading from the old market place to the Roebuck Inn" and with a compass, " a circle was described with a 3/4 mile radius."

This was unusual but not unique – what was different was the fact that the process was repeated in 1832 when Rochdale became a Parliamentary constituency, leaving the town with two circular boundaries.

14

BRITAIN'S MOST INFLUENTIAL TRADES UNION

A membership card for flannel weavers' union.

In 1834, six farm labourers from the village of Tolpuddle in Dorset were transported to Australia for belonging to a workers' organisation with a solemn binding oath. The secret "twisting-in" ceremony of these Tolpuddle Martyrs, it was later revealed, was borrowed from the Rochdale Journeymen Flannel Weavers' Association. Moreover, according to one of the first histories of the Trades Union Movement, this Rochdale Association devised "the best and simplest statement of the aims of the workers the age had produced."

Why was this Rochdale Union such a model of good practice for those that followed? The answer is partly in Rochdale's geographical location on the border of Lancashire and Yorkshire.

By the 1820's the town became the "Clearing House for Ideas" for the whole of the North of England. There was a long tradition of self-taught working people joining together to support one another in the quest to find solutions to the social upheaval caused by rapid industrial-isation.

One of the first local organisations fighting to retain a reasonable standard of living was the Journeymen Flannel Weavers' Association, formed when Trade Unions were still illegal in or around 1818. The foresight and determination of this early textile union influenced a later generation of weavers, many of whom would, in 1844, be involved in the Co-operative ventures of the Rochdale Pioneers.

LONGEST RESISTANCE TO AN ACT OF PARLIAMENT

BY THE 1830s the North of England had been transformed by the effects of industrialisation into the Workshop of the World.

In the South, agriculture still ruled – prone to seasonal economic chaos as bad harvests followed good.

In the bad years, thousands of unemployed farm labourers roamed the countryside "seeking shelter, casual labour or alms and horrifying the respectable classes."

In 1834 the Government passed the Poor Law Amendment Act. No more cash hand-outs for those out of work; no more almshouses providing temporary accommodation. In future the unemployed would be herded into giant Union workhouses predicted by Charles Dickens in *Oliver Twist*.

Fear was the key. Families were to be split up by age and gender and life inside the workhouse was to be so mercilessly hard as to deter all but the most desperate. This may have suited the landowners in the South. In the North in general, and in Rochdale in particular, the Act was received with horror – and fierce resistance. Rochdale's small workhouses provided shelter for those thrown out of work during the frequent slumps in the textile industry.

Inmates were generally treated with sympathy and respect. The contrast and approach between the North and South in workhouse administration is evident in the following extract from the unique diary of the Spotland workhouse master. In December 1836, a visitor from

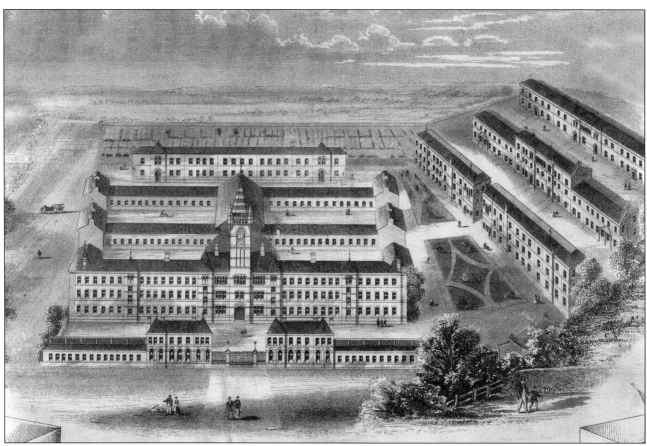

A picture of the "new" workhouse at Dearnley in 1877, better known now as Birch Hill Hospital.

London was received at Spotland – the governor of the massive St Giles Hospital Workhouse:

"He asked how did we keep so clear of bugs. We said that when they began to be troublesome the beds were taken down and cleaned and the rooms whitewashed. He asked if they (the inmates) had their meat weighed to them. We told him no they had as much set as they could eat and if they wanted more they had it."

The Act was to become law in 1837. In Rochdale mass protests were organised. Thousands of people crowded onto the Butts to hear speakers like local radical Thomas Livsey plead for common humanity in the treatment of the poor. Government commissioners visited the town demanding the construction of a single, giant "Union" workhouse. Livsey as Chairman of the Overseers refused to meet them.

They tried again ordering Livsey to meet them at 3 o'clock. Livsey failed to arrive, saying he didn't know if they meant the morning or the afternoon! The commissioners left.

Rochdale became the national centre of resistance to the hated Poor Law Amendment Act. Local political leaders fought the Act in Parliament and through the courts. MP John Fenton was unceremoniously ousted as Rochdale's representative for toeing his party's line and supporting the Act.

Eventually the Commissioners in London obtained an injunction forcing Rochdale to create the administrative framework for implementing the Act.

Although this edict was complied with, those elected to be the new Guardians of the Poor also refused to do more than meet occasionally and discuss general issues.

In the event, it was not until 1877, 43 years after the passing of the Poor Law Amendment Act, that Rochdale's single Union workhouse at Dearnley (now Birch Hill Hospital) was completed. A record for humanity and stubbornness unmatched anywhere else.

50 ROCHDALE RECORDS

16

THE WORLD'S FIRST RAILWAY TUNNEL

The magnificent viaduct at Healey Dell.

AS INDUSTRY expanded in the 19th century, a corresponding revolution in transport was essential. In the 1830's the Rochdale Canal and the new turnpike roads were not sufficient to accommodate the massive demands of trade and commerce.

The Engineers of the Manchester-Leeds railway,

Workmen at the entrance to the Summit Tunnel.

which was begun in 1839, were faced with the enormous challenge of negotiating the Summit Gap at Littleborough.

As the lower levels were too marshy and water-logged to sustain the weight of the railway, George Stephenson and his fellow engineers decided to excavate a tunnel 2,885 yards through solid rock at Summit.

Some 23 million bricks were used in an enterprise of mind-boggling ambition and typical Victorian bloody mindedness.

Huge numbers of navvies were employed as human machines scrambling and dynamiting through slabs of millstone grit.

Forty-one perished and hundreds more were injured. Their memorial was the Summit Tunnel - the longest railway tunnel in the world opened for public traffic in 1841.

Possibly Britain's most spectacular railway viaduct is at Healey Dell where tremendous stone piers, more than 100ft high, carry the former Rochdale-Bacup line over the River Spodden. A walkers' trail goes over the bridge and you can look down into an enormous bowl of trees that is the Healey Dell Nature Reserve.

The dramatic blaze that broke out in the tunnel in December 1984.

The members of the original Pioneers Society.

THE BIRTHPLACE OF THE CO-OP

JUST how important the work of those Rochdale Pioneers of

Co-operation was can be judged by the fact that today the movement has 700 million adherents worldwide – all acknowledging the "Rochdale Principles" of co-operation.

These principles, combining common sense and idealism, reflected the living conditions of ordinary people in the mid-1840's.

Rapid industrialisation

The first Co-op, now a museum, at Toad Lane.

The second Co-op branch which opened on Drake Street in 1865.

resulted in hunger, poverty, disease and widespread social unrest.

Working people, particularly weavers and other textile workers, evolved their own responses to these problems; developing organisations (including chapels), institutions and societies (including trade unions and burial societies).

One other society was that of the Rochdale Equitable Pioneers who, while providing reasonably-priced, unadulterated food for its members, devised a set of principles including:

● Democratic control of the organisation.

● One member, one vote.
● Equality of the sexes.
● Open membership.
● Political and religious neutrality.
● Education for all.
● Profits divided pro-rata depending upon the amount spent – The Divi!

The Pioneers began trading from 33 Toad Lane in December 1844.

The repercussions are still being felt today in Japan, the USA, South America and throughout Europe and Asia.

Co-operation places power

The new headquarters of the Co-operative Retail Society, which brought the Co-op back to Rochdale in 1996.

in the hands of ordinary people and provides educational opportunities, employment and a way of life for millions regardless of geographical or religious boundaries.

The Co-operative movement led to several other records recounted elsewhere; one that isn't is the world's first commercial production of marmalade, which we also believe occurred in Rochdale!

友貞 安太郎

ロッチデイル物語

近代協同組合運動の起こりと原則の成り立ち

ROCHDALE STORY

コープ出版

ロッチデイル
公正先駆者組合誕生150周年

21世紀に向かう世界の協同組合が、
いまこそ学ばなくてはならない「協同の精神」。
すべての協同組合人に贈る物語。

This Japanese book shows how people around the world remain interested in the start of Co-operation in Rochdale.

50 ROCHDALE RECORDS

18

BRITAIN'S ONLY CANAL BARGE PUB

WHAT do you do with a redundant canal barge? One possibility is to follow the example of an enterprising 19th century Rochdalian – drag it on to dry land and convert it into a pub!

The story of The Boat Inn, Belfield (also known as Uncle Tom's Cabin) begins in or around 1839 following the completion of the Manchester-Leeds Railway as far as Rochdale.

In those days Heywood had no rail link, so those wishing to travel to and from Castleton were forced to make the journey by canal. One of the boats which ferried passengers along this route was retired from active service in 1841 to become not only the Boat Inn

but also the Belfield Road toll house!

To achieve this transformation, the boat was roofed over with slate and the sides encased by whitewashed brick.

Inside, the pub remained very much a boat, complete with portholes and bulwarks. Amazingly, the interior contained a bar, kitchen, bar parlour, taproom and three bedrooms!

The Boat Inn also had its own brewhouse adjacent to the converted barge. Unsurprisingly, landlord Thomas Butterworth became known far and wide as "Tom o'th'Boat".

The Boat Inn, or Uncle Tom's Cabin.

THE FIRST GEOLOGY TRAIL

IN THE unlikely setting of Rochdale Cemetery is a remarkable creation; probably the first geology trail in the world.

In 1855, when the cemetery opened, geology was still a relatively young science. It seems that two enthusiasts – James Horsfall and Robert Law – who had helped plan the cemetery used the opportunity to construct a unique guide to the past.

The trail, almost all of which still survives, runs from one end of the cemetery to the other, composed of large slabs of different rocks; some gathered locally, some brought from further afield and even from overseas.

There are 26 sample stones, plus Start and Finish Stones; the former bearing the words

"In the beginning God created the Heaven and the Earth. "The series of pillars commencing here with Lava and, in the ascending order, terminating with Boulder Stones, elucidates their arrangement of the strata of the Earth's crust in the order they were formed by the Creator "Of old hast thou lain the foundations of the Earth."

The trail begins with basalt columns from the Giants' Causeway in Northern Ireland and continues via granite from Aberdeen and marble from Carrara in Italy.

There is black marble from Galway, Portland Stone from the Isle of Wight and green porphyrite from North Wales as well as sandstones from local quarries.

Ironically, the rock that Horsfall and Law thought was oldest is in fact the youngest!

Geologists Arthur Baldwin and Don Alderson who have researched the trail say that only two specimens have been lost; presumably through the effects of acid rain on the soft stone.

One of the stones in Rochdale's unique geology trail. Many visitors to the cemetery assume they are gravestones.

50 ROCHDALE RECORDS
20

INVENTOR OF THE MODERN CRICKET BALL

SPORT it has to be admitted is not an area in which Rochdale has excelled. Maybe it's something in the water but, with one or two notable exceptions, the town's sportsmen and women have not set the world alight. After all, Jack McAvoy boxing's "Rochdale Thunderbolt" was born in Burnley.

Sporting entries in Rochdale's local history books thus range from the trivial to the downright bizarre:

1878, Sept.16 Athletics: Maday Angelo walked 1,000 miles in 1,000 hours in a field near the Fox Inn.

1858, Sept.9. Cricket: XXII of Rochdale v England XI begun at Merefield. Hurt, one of XI, killed by a train walking to the station.

There is, however, one sporting record for the town to celebrate. In the 1860s Rochdale's Hamlet Nicholson presented the world with the first compound cricket ball and the snappily titled "Areekta Spiras" ball became the model for all those that followed.

50 ROCHDALE RECORDS
21

THE FIRST WAR PHOTOGRAPHER

ROGER Fenton was the son of Rochdale's first MP who went out to the Crimea with his camera and in doing so became the world's first war photographer.

The Ordnance Wharf at Balaclava. This picture shows something of the back-up required to fight a campaign like the Crimean War.

Fenton's images from the war brought this far away conflict into the sitting rooms of Victorian England. The war also saw the emergence of Florence Nightingale and of William Howard the Times' war correspondent who told the story of the Charge of the Light Brigade.

Fenton himself was born in 1819 and brought up in the family home at Crimble Hall, Bamford.

Fenton's famous informal portrait of Victoria and Albert.

first accredited war photographer. He travelled the area in a purpose-built studio – a converted shack drawn by horse.

All his pictures – mainly posed because of the limitations of photography at the time – were developed from wet prints; even in the heart of the battlefield.

Mr Stables says: "He didn't take many pictures of the blood and gore of battle, but that was probably because photography was in its infancy. He took 360 pictures of the war, including the soldiers and generals, and wrote 21 letters which can now be seen in the context of reports from the front line.

"There can be little doubt that Fenton had effectively earned himself the title of first-ever war correspondent."

Mr Stables adds: "In 1856 he gave a lecture about his photographic adventures at the public hall in Baillie Street, near what is now Telegraph House. He died aged 50 in 1869."

Historian Ron Stables says: "Fenton was a Rochdale lad who went to Paris in 1840 to study art and it was here that he became interested in the new art of photography; though when he returned to England he studied law and became a barrister.

"In 1847 he joined a photographic club in London and became secretary of the London Photographic Club which later became known as the Royal Photographic Society of Great Britain."

In 1854 he went out the Crimean War as the world's

ROCHDALE TOWN HALL – THE FINEST IN ENGLAND (with the best modern stained glass in the country)

THESE things are subjective of course, but internally and externally Rochdale's gothic Town Hall buildings rate as among the finest in Britain – never mind in the North.

For a start you can stand back and admire it in in all its glory. Rochdale Town Hall is no hidden gem dwarfed by high-rise concrete; the impossibility of building on the Esplanade river covering ensures that W.H. Crosland's magnum opus stands today as splendidly isolated as the architect intended.

Legend has it that Adolf Hitler had his eye on the stained glass – as well he might. Those who wish to see the finest modern stained glass in the country will find it in Rochdale Town Hall. But the Town Hall has, over the years, had its ups and downs.

The first "up" – and up, and up – was the cost. Crosland's original tender of £20,000 proved to be a massive underestimate. As the architect's ambition soared so did the price. When, in 1871, he got to the £150,000 mark, despairing councillors ordered a halt. Consequently the decoration in the Small Exchange remains unfinished to this day and in the old Reception Room, Councillor Edward Taylor, immortalised in stone, shakes his fist in perpetuity at the unrepentent architect.

The first "down" was the original wooden-topped spire which scraped the clouds at a breathtaking 240 feet. In 1883 dry rot was found and, in attempting to dismantle the top portion, workmen may or may not have tried to speed the process with the help of a match or two. Whatever the cause, on 10 April 1883, the spire burned nearly to the ground in front of an excited crowd of sightseers.

The best efforts of the Rochdale and Oldham fire brigade were in vain. Early on, the sight of the horse-drawn Rochdale appliance charging round and round the blazing buildings in order to get steam up for their pumps must have been a source of great entertainment. The arrival of the Heywood brigade on the following morning has become the stuff of legend.

The Council turned to Alfred Waterhouse, the architect of Manchester Town Hall, to replace the tower. His more sober stone edifice, finished in 1887, may not be as much fun as Crosland's sublime folly but complements the main body of the building and completes what is, without a doubt, the finest Town Hall in the North of England.

The Magnificent main stairway and stained glass in Rochdale Town Hall.

WHERE WOMEN WON PROPERTY RIGHTS

ONCE again Rochdale owes this claim to fame to the Rochdale Pioneers and the early Co-operative movement.

Before 1870, a married woman's property – money, land, everything – belonged legally to her husband. The Rochdale Pioneers, with their principle of Equality of Membership, made no distinction between the sexes. If a man queried his wife's financial status within the organisation he was refused any information and the woman was told of his enquiry.

When the Home Secretary of the time was investigating this issue, he dispatched his Private Secretary, Albert Rutson, to Rochdale. Rutson was so impressed by what he saw in Rochdale that, despite the Pioneers operating, strictly speaking, outside the law he reported back positively to the Home Secretary.

When the Married Woman's Property Act was finally passed in 1870, it was largely due to Rutson's conversion by the Rochdale Pioneers.

WORLD'S LARGEST PRIVATELY-OWNED NURSERY

THOUSANDS of Rochdale people have fond memories of Bright's Nursery on Whitworth

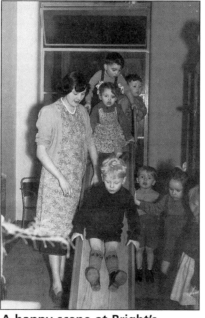

A happy scene at Bright's Nursery.

Road, but how many know that when it first opened it was the largest privately-run day nursery in the world?

The firm of John Bright and Brothers had operated a nursery as far back as 1875 – one of the earliest examples in the country – and had also run a day school for the children of its workforce. However, they were modest facilities compared with the handsomely equipped premises opened on 10 January 1950.

The Nursery and adjacent play area covered "a total of 4,000 square yards and was designed to cater for 168 babies and children up to school age." Twenty three nursing staff supported by ten domestic staff were employed to run the centre, "and the charge to parents was 7s 6d per week." Revealingly, although nursery provision is still not widely available in the workplace today, in 1950 Bright's considered the nursery "a real necessity".

When John Bright and Brothers ceased trading, their famous nursery was acquired by Rochdale's Social Services Department and is still used as a day care centre for babies and toddlers.

THE LAST PACKHORSE DRIVER

THE Pennine hills were for centuries the domain of the packhorse; the steep gradients and the boggy moorland being unsuited for almost any other form of transport until the coming of the canals, railways and turnpike roads.

Most goods were carried on teams of horses which plied their way between the Pennine towns on a special, hardy breed of pony known as the "Galloway".

Lime from the Ribble Valley was a major commodity, used to sweeten acid soils, limewash buildings and make cement. As a consequence the ponies were known as "lime gals" and the trackway over the moors from Burnley towards Rochdale as "Limersgate".

Our moors still abound with packhorse routes – some still with their original stone flags – and the easily recognised packhorse bridges which are too narrow for any other form of transport. In the days when people moved around little, the packhorse drivers were one of the main sources of news and gossip; their coming announced by the jingling of their packhorse bells (two sets of which are in the Rochdale Museum collection).

The drivers themselves were often colourful characters and Ailse o' Fussers, the last of them, was certainly one of these. Legend has it that, in a surprisingly modern touch, she had a young farmer as her "toy boy"!

William Robertson in his book "*Rochdale and the Vale of Whitworth*" refers to Ailse – her full name was Mary Alice Hartley – as follows:

"In her palmy days she had as many as 20 gals and they carried bags of coal from Land Coalpit near Shawforth and sometimes lime from Clitheroe and Burnley. They travelled the pack horse roads from Cliviger to Bacup along the foot of Brown Wardle; down Cronkeyshaw into Rochdale." Remarkably the picture we show here is dated 1877.

The redoubtable Ailse o' Fussers, still taking goods on pony back in 1877.

THE STREET MADE OF WOOD

WHEN Rochdale's first hospital was established at King Street, off South Parade, the street was paved with wooden setts, not the traditional stone ones. This was so that patients would not be disturbed by the noise of horses and carriages using the street.

The wooden setts still survive to this day and some can be seen peeping through a gap in the tarmac which now covers them.

Perhaps a section of this unique street should be properly revealed and covered in glass or Perspex so that it remains open to view while safe from damage.

The unusual wooden setts on King Street.

THE LONGEST ROW IN THE WORLD?

MOSS Row at Norden was certainly the longest terrace by far in Rochdale and we've been unable to come up with any other row of traditional workers' houses anywhere else that comes near to equalling it.

Mr H.Swain,of Spotland Tops, Cutgate, tells us that he has happy memories of being brought up there in the 1930s and is sad that the 1970s saw the row being flattened for a by-pass that was never built.

He says: "Although there were 40 houses, there were 41 chimneys, the reason being that the first house in the row had two front rooms downstairs, so it had two fireplaces".

Mr Swain's brother, who lives at College Bank, Rochdale, says that Moss Row was more usually known as "Long Row".

He says: "About a quarter of the way up the row was the local shop. I think the family who ran it were Mr and Mrs Kay."

He adds: "One of the tricks the kids got up to in those days was to turn on the taps on the milkman's containers while he was delivering to the houses. With the row being on a bit of a slope, all you could see would be a river of milk on its way down the road with the kids looking on from the distance, where the milkman couldn't see them."

FISH AND CHIPS ON WHEELS—JAMES NUTTALL, FATHER OF FAST FOOD

NOT the biggest firm in Rochdale, but certainly one of the best known, was Henry Nuttall Ltd whose fish and chip ranges could – and still can – be found the length and breadth of the country.

The firm grew from a small back street shop run by an ex-blacksmith to be an inter-national firm.

Fried fish was widely available in the 1830s. Dickens has his characters dining on take-away fish in "Great Expectations". Fried potatoes go back even further. Which genius began cutting potatoes into chips and serving them with fried fish in batter is, unfortunately, not recorded.

Oldham, it has been claimed, was the first town where fish and chips took off in a big way. There was no doubt, however, that it was James Nuttall of Rochdale, who by inventing the fish and chip range, created the world's first fast food industry.

It was in or around 1872 that Nuttall of Dane Street, a gasfitter and tinmaker began constructing his mighty chip ranges (including an extremely volatile horse-drawn version). Having patented his invention Nuttall began to make an exceptionally good living out of fast food – so good that his son John went into competition with him.

When James Nuttall died his executors continued trading as "the old and original firm". John, meanwhile, describing himself as the son of the original patentee, declared, "I am absolutely the oldest practical maker in the trade

A mobile fish and chip range made by Nuttall's.

mud of Flanders with chips for the troops.

The firm moved to Holmes Street shortly before the second world war and during that time used its engineering skills to make aircraft parts; especially for the Halifax bomber.

Britain's first nuclear submarine, Dreadnought, put to sea with a Nuttall range on board. In later years the firm exported ranges to Canada and America.

In one deal, a Canadian chain of English-style pubs bought ranges with decorative panels featuring Lancashire scenes including Rochdale Town Hall.

But, in 1980, the firm closed. It was later re-opened after a takeover, but a further takeover in 1995 saw the firm then based at Regent Street moved to Sheffield.

having no connection with any other firm using the name J. Nuttall in Rochdale." So there!

It was John Nuttall's premises in Bridge Street that was acquired by Henry Nuttall around 1916 and it was Henry who steered the firm during its years of expansion in the 1920s and '30s. It was also Henry who stated memorably,

"No cheaper or more wholesome food than chips has ever been in the reach of the working class." We remain in his debt!

In the First World War, determined that British soldiers should not miss out on their favourite dish, the firm produced horse-drawn ranges which ploughed through the

50 ROCHDALE RECORDS

29

HOME OF THE FLAGSTONE WALL

JOHN Ruskin, author, art critic and founder of Ruskin College, Oxford, visited Rochdale in 1859. He was not overly impressed.

Describing the House in the Wood, which stood on the site of the present Town Hall, Ruskin recalled: "*Just outside the town I came across an old English cottage or mansion, set close under the hill and beside the river ...with mullioned windows and a low-arched porch ...the garden cruelly blighted utterly into a field of ashes ...the roof torn into shapeless rents; the shutters hanging about the windows in rags of rotten wood; before the gate the stream ...black as ebony,thick with curdling scum*

...the furnaces of the city foaming forth perpetual plague of sulphurous darkness; the volumes of their storm clouds coiling low over a waste of grassless fields, fenced from each other not by hedges but by slabs of square stone, like gravestones, riveted together with iron."

These flagstone walls of millstone grit exist elsewhere but are undoubtedly far more common in Rochdale where they can be seen, even today, in great numbers.

Flagstone "fences" like this are more common in and around Rochdale than anywhere else. Made of "seconds" created when flagstones were being hewn from local quarries, they are held together by pieces of iron.

THE SPIRITUAL HOME OF ADULT EDUCATION

THE Rochdale Pioneers and all the local Co-operators who followed them saw education as the lifeline for ordinary people — the key to self-improvement and self-respect.

By 1877 the Rochdale Society supported 14 libraries throughout the town, all dedicated to the cause of adult education. In the 20 years that followed, many members became dedicated to the concept of University Extension Classes whereby working people could attend lectures and tutorials in their own town.

Albert Mansbridge, an employee of the Co-operative Wholesale Society, devised a new approach to adult education by proposing a partnership of the Universities, Trades Unions and Co-operative Societies. In 1903 he founded the Worker's Educational Association (WEA) to which Co-operative Societies were asked to affiliate and in 1905 the Rochdale Equitable Pioneers became the second society to join the movement.

Although not the first to join up, because of the Pioneers original contribution and because the Rochdale branch was the most active and enlightened in the country, Mansbridge always viewed Rochdale as the spiritual home of the WEA – an organisation which flourishes in the town to this day.

A class at Rochdale Art School in the antique room in 1907. One of the fruits of the drive to develop adult education.

41

31

THE WIDEST BRIDGE IN THE WORLD

THE 19th century saw Rochdale transformed from a "fine stone-built market town" into a grimy, polluted industrial centre.

Its river, the Roch, once crystal clear, oozed thick with dye, candle tallow, effluent and garbage.

The smell invaded nearby buildings, mingling with the smoke from the factories and coke-burning fires.

Access over the river was via the 17th century Rochdale Bridge, or the smaller Walk Bridge and later over Captain Ogden's Bridge to the old House in the Wood (on the site of the present Town Hall).

As if the animal carcasses floating downstream were not enough, the advent of the snorting, clanging steam trams in the 1880's presented further difficulties.

The old bridge was not broad enough or strong enough to allow the trams to pass from Drake Street to the commercial sector on the other side of the river.

The council therefore resolved to cover and culvert the river. This was achieved in sections between 1904 and 1926 stretching from Smith Street to the far end of the present Esplanade.

A major feat of engineering, this ferro-concrete structure has a total width of 1460 feet and is to all intents and purposes a bridge, formerly the widest in the world, but still certainly the widest in Europe.

The view downstream from Wellington Bridge after flooding in 1903 as work began on covering the River Roch.

WORLD'S FIRST EARTHQUAKE EXPERT

IT IS a strange fact that a local man, born in 1850 and nicknamed "Earthquake Milne', is still revered today in Japan. John Milne was brought up at 147 Drake Street, Rochdale and at Tunshill, Milnrow – where his family originated.

He received his early education at what he referred to as "Miss Fisher's, Milkstone Road" but from what appears a fairly unpromising start, Milne went on to become the world's greatest seismologist. For over twenty years he had been employed by the Japanese Government as a geologist and mining engineer then, because, as he himself said: "in Japan you have earthquakes for breakfast, earthquakes for lunch and earthquakes for tea", he became fascinated by the then primitive science of seismology.

Almost entirely as a result of Milne's dedication and foresight, the Seismic Study of Japan was instigated with a network of 968 recording stations throughout the country. Milne, who is credited with inventing the modern seismograph (which maps and records earthquake activity) also had some success in the extremely difficult task of predicting where and when earth tremors would occur. As a result, in addition to being awarded a professorship at Tokyo University, Milne was showered with honours both in Japan and by the Royal Society in Britain.

Modern earthquake science owes a massive debt to Milne. Because of his early warning systems predicting earthquake activity, many people around the world indirectly owe him their lives. So it is not so surprising after all, that, although he died as long ago as 1913, John Milne enjoys hero-status in Japan to this day.

John "Earthquake" Milne.

33

THE NORTH'S FIRST FACTORY CANTEEN

FACILITIES for the workers in early factories were virtually non-existent. You went there to work; you ate by your machine, in the yard or on a stairwell; you went home.

It was not until the beginning of the 20th century that a few more enlightened firms were providing modern facilities for their workers and factory canteens had been started in a number of larger firms.

However, Rochdale machine manufacturers, Thomas Robinson's, are credited with establishing the first factory canteen in the North as far back as 1881.

As the Rochdale Observer reported on 17 December of that year: "For some time in the factory there has been a room for those men to dine whose homes were too distant to go home for dinner. The new Railway Works Coffee Tavern has now been created in its stead.

"The downstairs contains tables for 200 with kitchen and large bar. Upstairs has accommodation for 700 people and is to be used for meetings, concerts etc."

Robinson's, which closed in Rochdale in 1986 after 148 years in the town, has yet another claim to fame. In 1877 the engineering works covered 7 acres and employed 1200 people – at that time, the largest concern of its kind in the world.

34

MOST MONKEY PUZZLES AT THE LAST TEA GARDENS

THE aptly-named Monkey Puzzle trees – or Chile Pines to give them their proper name – were with their peculiar foliage popular features of many Edwardian and Victorian gardens.

Millcroft Tea Gardens, at Norden, boasts the largest collection of such trees in the North of England; an amazing 28 of them.

They were planted by Mr Lee, a Norfolk market gardener, who came here at the turn of the century planting fruit, vegetables and ornamental trees and shrubs. But competing with growers in more climatically favoured Cheshire meant it was always a tough battle and his wife began making and selling teas to eke out their living.

In 1914, the gardens were taken over by a Bury glove shop owner who decided to concentrate on the teas side of the business and built a small shed at the side of the house in which they could be served.

People flocked to Millcroft and among the attractions were giant swing boats which must have given it a fairground atmosphere.

In a day when mill workers were discovering the delights of the countryside there was a great demand for places like Millcroft, selling refreshments in countryside areas close to centres of population. Tea rooms and tea gardens sprung up by the dozen – you can still

Some of the monkey puzzle trees at Millcroft Tea Gardens.

One of the last survivors, the tearooms themselves.

see the sign of the old Carr Wood tea rooms on a building less than a mile away.

As tastes became more sophisticated and transport less of a problem, they gradually died and few are left. The Millcroft Tea Gardens are possibly the best surviving example, still serving food and drinks every Sunday and on holidays.

Of the swing boats only the rusting remnants remain, but the grounds are still a paradise of flowers looked over by the dark strands of the monkey puzzle trees.

Since 1929 the gardens have been in the care of the Leach family who maintain a fascinating collection of local memorabilia. Outside are stone carvings of Judge Jefferies and Britannia, from the old Strangeways courts in Manchester; two ornamental pots from Norden House; a carving from the spire of Rochdale Town Hall which burned down in 1880.

The tearoom, enlarged since its earliest days, features antique furniture and a famous "rogue" badger which had wreaked havoc in the surrounding countryside until it was hunted down, killed and stuffed.

Walkers and cyclists come from miles around to enjoy the beautiful countryside of the Ashworth Valley and to drink not only a cup of tea but also drink in a piece of living history.

35

ONLY ROYAL INFIRMARY THAT ISN'T 'ROYAL'

IF A hospital was opened by, or graced with a plaque-unveiling ceremony from, the reigning monarch, it was entitled to be officially identified as a Royal Infirmary. This applied if the royal visitor opened a major extension or a new wing, so Oldham's Infirmary is called, obviously, "Oldham Royal Infirmary".

However, although in 1913 King George V and Queen Mary unveiled a plaque officially opening the extension to Rochdale Infirmary, the hospital is not recognised as a "Royal Infirmary". Why? The answer is that the opening ceremony was done by remote control! Due to an extremely busy schedule the royal couple did not cross the hospital threshold but instead pressed a button on a rostrum in the Town Hall Square. This created an electric current which virtually simultaneously activated a mechanism for unveiling the plaque in the Infirmary. Heath Robinson would undoubtedly have approved but as a result we have plain old Rochdale Infirmary!

36

THE WORLD'S LARGEST FACTORY UNDER ONE ROOF

The Dunlop Mills under construction.

ROCHDALE'S first generation woollen mills were comparatively small.

They were clustered initially around the fast-flowing Pennine streams and it was not until the 1830s that steam overtook water power as the primary source of energy for local factories.

In 1838, the 117 mills of the Rochdale area employed an average only 90 people. By way of contrast, the mere 44 mills of Blackburn sustained an average of 240 workers.

Twenty years later and George Ashworth, the owner of Rochdale's largest factory, employed 900 people – large by Rochdale's standards but modest compared with the giant structures of Oldham and Bolton.

Even in the late 19th century when the limited companies began to replace the old family firms, it was Oldham which led the way in the construction of red brick super mills.

Then, in 1916, the Dunlop Rubber Company purchased an existing mill site in Rochdale to create a vast 33-acre complex of spinning and weaving sheds.

In his inaugural speech, William Pilling chairman of the local board of directors, thanked Dunlop for establishing in Rochdale " a factory with 250,000 ring spindles, 107,000 drawing spindles, 580 looms employing 3,200 people – the world's largest factory under one roof".

A view showing the massive extent of the completed factory.

37

MOST CONSISTENTLY UNSUCCESSFUL LEAGUE FOOTBALL SIDE
(but the great survivors)

SINCE 1921, when both were elected to the Football League, Rochdale and Hartlepool have been locked in a battle for this title. Rochdale's best league position (ninth in the old Division Three) is better than Hartlepool can claim and Dale's six seasons out of the bottom flight is also better than Hartlepool's. But it is a near thing and Hartlepool can claim to have had an international in their team, unlike Rochdale, and their FA Cup record is consistently less bad (better would be stretching the word too far).

Torquay United, a possible rival, have only been in the league since 1927 and once managed to attain the giddy heights of fourth in the former Division Three.

Exeter City made it to a best position of eighth in this division, but have had an almost respectable 17 seasons out of the bottom division.

Sides like Crewe, Stockport and Tranmere, which once might have given Rochdale competition, have enjoyed great success in recent seasons.

Wigan Athletic, only elected to the league in 1978, have already managed more seasons out of the basement than Rochdale. Peterborough (elected in 1960) can recall a time in the new First Division, while Hereford who arrived only in 1972 and are now back in non-league action managed to get one season in the old Division Two.

Other rivals like Chester, Chesterfield, Colchester, Darlington, Doncaster, Gillingham, Hereford, Lincoln, Mansfield, Peterborough, Southend, Shrewsbury, Wigan and York can all claim greater "highs" and more years out of football's basement.

Some minnows like Carlisle and Northampton can even claim a season in the top flight, the old Division One.

Many can claim at least a few seasons in the old Division Two, current Division One.

But Rochdale's great claim is that they have never been ejected from the league, either by failing re-election or through relegation.

Even Burnley, League champions in 1959/60 and FA Cup winners and finalists have come closer to the trapdoor, needing to win their last match of a season to survive.

Doncaster Rovers (best position seventh in the old Division Two) are the latest Football League club to leave the fold. Hopefully, like Darlington, Lincoln and Halifax (three other members of football's list of under-achievers) who also suffered this fate, they will return.

Meanwhile Rochdale maintain a record that is equally remarkable for survival as it is for lack of success.

Rochdale FC's Spotland Ground; one that has seen very few great days.

38

FROM ROCHDALE TO HARVARD

JOSHUA Whatmough was born in a two-room, waterless cottage in June , 1897. His mother was a weaver and his father an iron moulder.

From the earliest age it was clear that young Joshua was an exceptional child. At the age of three he could read perfectly and often entertained folk by reading from whatever book they chose to put before him.

It was an achievement gained against remarkable odds. When the headmaster of the local school came to announce to his parents that Joshua had a brilliant scholarly talent, his parents replied that "they would beat it out of him".

In spite of this he went on to win a scholarship to Manchester University with the choice of reading either Classics or Mathematics. He chose the former.

From 1921 to 1925 he lectured on Greek and Latin in North Wales, before going to the Egyptian University at Cairo to teach French. It is said that he kept a revolver in his desk at this time as a precaution.

In 1926 he went to Harvard where he became Professor of Comparative Philology. A remarkable rise for someone from such humble origins.

39

THE LARGEST WORKING MILL ENGINE IN THE WORLD

AT MILNROW, alongside the M62 motorway, stands a lonely brick building quite obviously left over from being part of a large cotton mill.

Less obvious to those rushing past is that inside is the largest working mill engine in the world; something that has to be seen to be believed and which – thanks to the efforts of the Ellenroad Trust – can be both seen and believed. The engine is enormous, the fly-wheel alone weighs as much as nine double deck buses and is 28ft in diameter. It is capable of producing 3,000 horse power.

Built by John McNaught of Rochdale in 1890, the engine powered the Ellenroad spinning mill until 1916 when the original mill was destroyed by one of the all-too frequent fires which plagued the cotton industry.

In 1920 the mill was rebuilt as a modern ring spinning plant and the engine modified to give more power.

It ran in this form until 1975, by which time it was one of the last great steam engines to power a mill. The giant 270,000 sq ft mill which was powered by the engine was unfortunately demolished in the 1980s, but new owners Coates Brothers Inks joined a partnership to save and preserve the engine which was scheduled by English Heritage as an industrial monument.

The engine can be seen in all its working glory the first Sunday of every month (January excepted), when it is in steam from noon to 4pm.

Many thousands of people enjoy watching steam locomotives, but only a fraction of that number visit working mill engines. They don't know what they are missing; for even the non-mechanical minded the sight of the great wheels, the shining metalwork, the pistons and the countless smaller moving parts are truly – as the Trust itself proclaims – "a symphony of polished brass and steel".

50 ROCHDALE RECORDS

FIRST FIRE ENGINES OUTSIDE LONDON WITH TWO-WAY RADIOS

IN 1825 the Rochdale Police Act empowered local commissioners to " police and watch the town". These powers extended to the provision of fire-fighting equipment.

A pamphlet of the rules of the early "Rochdale Police Firemen" reveals that the keys of the engine house behind the Workhouse were kept, with one protective helmet, next door to the Mount Pleasant Tavern. No temptation there then!

Rochdale's Police Fire Brigade remained poorly equipped. In 1857 there were only hand pumps, superceded later by manual engines. The acquisition of a steam fire engine, capable of throwing a jet of water of 220 feet, did not prevent the conflagration of 1883 which destroyed the original Town Hall spire – despite the fire service being based in the building!

In 1893 the Fire Station was removed to Alfred Street where six horses and two steam engines were housed. Here, the stable doors were opened by an ingenious device " which simultaneously released the halters from the horses' heads - ensuring the fastest possible response."

Prior to the opening of the new Maclure Road station, the brigade introduced a number of innovations. The most noteworthy of these came in 1927 when the fire engines were fitted with two-way wireless systems – the second force in the country and the first outside London to be so equipped.

50 ROCHDALE RECORDS

THE FIRST MODERN SPORTS PATRON

IN 1927 the *Rochdale Observer* described a local man of humble origins as "the most dominating and spectacular personality who had any connection with the town".

Virtually forgotten now, Jimmy White was the forerunner of today's wealthy sports patrons like Jack Walker at Blackburn and John Hall at Newcastle. Born in Sun Place, Rochdale in 1877, Jimmy White amassed his fortune firstly as a builder, then as a mortgage broker and finally as a property and financial speculator.As Chairman of the Beecham Trust he purchased the entire town of Shaftesbury and sold it for a massive profit a few days later; he then negotiated the purchase of the prime-site Covent Garden Estate and casually bought and sold Selfridge's World Famous department store in the same week.

His personal wealth financed his passion for gambling, horseracing, boxing and particularly cricket. Although over the years he lavished many gifts on Rochdale Football Club, it was Rochdale Cricket Club to which White contributed the most time, energy and money.

Determined that the town should have the best league cricket side in the country, White approached the finest professional of the day, Cecil Parkin, persuaded him to move to Rochdale and financed several seasons at Rochdale out of his own pocket. Under White's patronage Rochdale Cricket Club topped the Central Lancashire League from 1922 to 1925 inclusive and again in 1927.

However in that year White's luck finally ran out when he was responsible for a disastrous deal with the Spies Petroleum Company which left the Beecham Trust with a deficit of over £1million. Preferring, it was said, death to dishonour, White committed suicide on 28 July 1927.

The millionaire Jimmy White (front centre) flanked by boxers (among them Bombardier Billy Wells) at a fund-raising, exhibition boxing match for Rochdale Cricket Club in 1921.

50 ROCHDALE RECORDS

42

THE HIGHEST-PAID MOVIE STAR

YES, she was the world's highest-paid female movie star!

Rochdale's singing sensation Gracie Fields - Our Gracie took the *Yankee Dollar* and signed a Hollywood contract which put all other female performers in the shade.

Gracie, born in 1898, shot from youthful obscurity at the Circus and Hippodrome, Rochdale, to stardom in the British cinema via music hall and variety.

Her success in the 1937 film *We're Going to be Rich*, prompted Hollywood mogul Darryl F Zanuck, to offer Gracie £200,000 for a four picture deal - a fortune in those days and more than Mae West (at the time America's highest paid actress) was earning.

The Rochdale-born lass who was the highest-paid female movie star in the world now has her own Web site on the Internet. (www.rochdale.gov.uk/gracie)

The newly-made CBE Gracie Fields in 1938 at the gates of Buckingham Palace.

43

BRITAIN'S MOST NOTORIOUS HANGMAN

OF ALL those who had the dubious honour of holding the position of Public Hangman, Huddersfield's Henry Pierrepoint is probably the best remembered. Rochdale's John Ellis, however, was the most notorious; largely because he recreated his gruesome role on stage and as a sideshow in a travelling fair.

Ellis, who was born in Broad Lane, Rochdale, worked in textiles and as a hairdresser before, "for reasons he could never explain", applying for the post of Public Hangman. During his grim career Ellis was responsible for dispatching George Smith (the so-called "Brides in the Bath" murderer), Crippen and Sir Roger Casement. Ellis resigned his post in 1924 largely as a reaction, some claim, to his

Hangman John Ellis with his stage show.

participation in the hanging of a woman – Edith Thompson.

Three years later Ellis was on his uppers and it was then that he recreated his hangman's role in a play dramatising the true life story of murderer Charles Pearce. When the venture flopped amidst a barrage of protest, Ellis retained the mock scaffold he had used in the theatre and began presenting "hangman shows" in travelling fairs. Unsurprisingly Ellis who suffered increasingly from depression, committed suicide in September 1932.

Ellis outside his hairdresser's shop in Oldham Road.

50 ROCHDALE RECORDS

44

THE FIRST TV ELECTION

Cameras roll in the first television by-election.

IT'S HARD to imagine now, but in the 1950s Rochdale was represented in Parliament by the Conservative Lt Colonel Wentworth Schofield helped by an informal agreement with the Liberals who had not put up a candidate in the previous election.

In return the Conservatives fielded no candidate in several seats where the Liberals had sitting MPs.

When the 66-year-old MP died in December, 1957 – only a few weeks after marrying a younger bride – this cozy agreement was ended and the stage set for one of the highest profile by-elections ever held in this country and, also, the first to be covered by television.

It wasn't just the Liberals' decision to field a candidate, but the fact that they picked a television personality, Ludovic Kennedy, whose wife was the glamorous film star and dancer Moira Shearer.

Such was the interest generated that Granada Television approached Rochdale's Town Clerk and asked to cover proceedings; not just the election itself but also staging two meet-the-candidate debates. The BBC, not to be left behind, also arrived in Rochdale, conducting interviews with passers-by outside the Town Hall.

Then came the Columbia Broadcasting Corporation which sent a camera team over from America as the by-election was arousing interest even there.

Kennedy enjoyed the lion's share of the publicity against his less glamorous rivals; Labour's John (Jack) McCann and the Conservatives' John Parkinson.

His TV background came to the fore in the way in which he created countless "photo opportunities"; not something that had been considered part of a candidate's duties up to that date.

His approach paid dividends. On polling day, 13 February, although the Labour man won with 22,000 votes, Kennedy's total of 17,603 was not too far behind and represented an enormous increase on any Liberal vote in Rochdale since the 1920s. The Tory limped in with less than 10,000 votes.

For better or for worse a new way of running election campaigns had arrived.

The Liberals did, of course, go on to win the Rochdale seat, and Sir Cyril Smith (as he was to become later) is probably the most famous backbench MP for many decades.

45

THE FIRST ALL-WEATHER MOTORWAY

WINTER motoring in the Pennines has always been a risky business. In Manchester and Leeds the weather may be mild, but less than a score of miles away the hill roads can be deep under snow and impassable.

Even the valley routes can suffer and, as Littleborough residents know only too well, when the moorland routes are closed the weight of traffic on the relatively low-level route through Summit and Todmorden becomes blocked by all the traffic.

Building a motorway across the very tops of the Pennines, between the summits of Blackstone Edge and Way Stone Edge, was therefore a major challenge; especially when it was claimed that this would be a route that should remain

The summit of the M62 motorway – the highest point on Britain's motorway network. Spanning the road is the Pennine Way footbridge.

open in almost every weather.

The careful design of the embankments, the cuttings and the gentle, contouring climb on either have made this prediction come true to a surprisingly high degree.

At Rakewood, at the top of Hollingworth Lake, one of the most challenging stretches of

the M62 can be seen.

The Rakewood Viaduct is 840ft long with 20 concrete columns carrying it 140ft above the valley bottom.

Work began on the viaduct in 1966 and it opened to motorway traffic in October, 1971.

BRITAIN'S FIRST COMMUNITY PRIMARY SCHOOL

THE seeds for Britain's first Community Primary School, opened at Belfield in 1973, were sown in Rochdale hundreds of years earlier. Education and self-education were always a local priority.

In 1770 one of the country's first subscription libraries - later known as Hartley's Library - opened in Stationer's Entry (still signposted) off the Butts. Everyone knows the massive contribution made by the Rochdale Pioneers to the development of Adult Education (see Number 30), then in 1870 Rochdale became one of the first four local authorities in the country to apply for powers to establish schools under the Education Act of that year (the Board Schools).

In 1967, the Plowden Report advocated closer links between schools and parents and the creation of a partnership between schools and the communities in which they were situated. In addition to the establishment of a meeting hall, coffee bar and a library on the school premises, Belfield was the first Primary School nationwide to elect a community council to co-ordinate and develop its facilities - and thus implement the Plowden Report's recommendations.

The various roles of the centre were summarised as follows: a branch library on afternoons and Saturday mornings, a study and information centre, a community information centre, a facility for clubs and community activities, a social centre, a mother and toddler's facility and a luncheon centre for the elderly.

Most of these services are still provided as Belfield celebrates 25 years as Britain's first community primary school.

Another milestone for Belfield was the nationally-famous Belfield Reading Project, the first of its type in the North of England. This involved the parents of children being advised how to assess their children's reading ability and organising a system of regularly sending children home with reading books. This unique partnership had a dramatic effect on reading standards.

The Belfield Community School netball team with parents and staff in 1978.

50 ROCHDALE RECORDS
47

BRITAIN'S FIRST AUTOMATIC TILLS ROCHDALE

ROCHDALE shoppers were the first in the country to have their groceries checked by automatic till scanners.

Bosses at the Asda headquarters in Leeds were divided over the introduction of the system, so the Nixon Street superstore at Castleton was chosen as a guinea pig in the early 1980s.

It was an instant success and within a matter of months Asda had converted all their stores to the scanning system.

50 ROCHDALE RECORDS
48

HOME RULE FOR CLOVERHALL

Cloverhall tenants sign the ground-breaking agreement to run their own estate.

IN 1985, the Cloverhall Tenants' Association Co-operative became the first council house tenants in the country to manage their own estate.

In the process they showed that the Co-operative principle is still alive and well in Rochdale.

The tenants have run the 243 home estate ever since, making successful bids for government funding which led to £3m of improvements in the late 1980s.

Before the tenants took over, the estate had large numbers of empty properties and a large repairs backlog. Now it is a pleasant and popular area to live.

49

THE BIGGEST PANCAKE IN THE WORLD

IN AUGUST 1994, Rochdale celebrated the 150th anniversary of the founding of the Co-operative movement by the famous Pioneers.

Among the attractions was a successful attempt, organised by Roger Baldry, to make, cook and flip the largest pancake in the world and more than 40,000 people packed the town centre to see it. But it wasn't all plain sailing. A tanker poured pancake mix into the 50ft diameter pan with giant gas burners below, but the mixture stubbornly refused to cook through under the watching lenses of cameras from TV's *Recordbreakers* programme.

The appropriate time for flipping came and went with the top of the pancake still runny. It was hours after the designated time that the giant

Hosepipes pump out the pancake batter.

creation was finally ready to be hoisted aloft by enormous cranes and flipped from its

pan. Anxious officials from Rochdale Council's Trading Standards and Environmental

Health sections monitored the entire process and pronounced that the operation had met Guinness Book of Record standards.

The old record had been broken by 8 feet. The pancake was later cut into 15,000 portions and sold at 25p each to raise money for local charities.

The giant pancake is "flipped".

50 ROCHDALE RECORDS

50

MORE "HOME-GROWN" STARS THAN ANY TOWN OF COMPARABLE SIZE

EVERYONE knows Gracie Fields hailed from Rochdale, but did you know all of these people did too?

Lisa Stansfield Rochdale soul-singing sensation.

Kaleef, the rapping Asian combo.

Tim Bobbin, father of Lancashire dialect writing (featured elsewhere).

James Kay-Shuttleworth, renowned welfare and health reformer whose campaigning led him to become acknowledged as the father of free education for all.

Trevor Hoyle, writer/novelist. He wrote episodes of *Blakes*

Norman Evans.

Seven as well as many well-received novels and award-winning plays.

Roger Fenton, the first war photographer (featured elsewhere).

Norman Evans, Music Hall star of *Over the Garden Wall* fame.

Walter Kershaw, artist whose speciality is murals on house or factory walls.

Karen and Marcus Hilton, National Ballroom Dance champions on many occasions.

Christine Gaskell, 1974 Commonwealth gold medalist at swimming.

A Walter Kershaw mural at South Street, Wardle.

Rochdale's rapping Asian combo, Kaleef.

G.H.Elliott, black-face singer of the 1930s and 40s. Born in 1882 at the George and Dragon Inn in Blackwater Street, he was famous as "The Chocolate Coloured Coon", a name he would be unlikely to have used today! He died in 1962.

Andy and Liz Kershaw, Radio One disc jockeys, the former famous as a World Music buff, radio personality and traveller.

Kieran Prenderville, *That's Life* presenter and creator of *Ballykissangel*.

John Bright and fellow anti-Corn Law campaigner Richard Cobden.

Sir Cyril Smith, the most famous back bench MP.

David Taylor, TV's *Zoo Vet*.

Zoo Vet David Taylor.

Colin Baker, actor and the second "Baker" to play *Doctor Who*.

Andrew Nutter, TV chef.

James Leach, leading Methodist hymn writer (featured elsewhere).

John Bright, the most famous

reforming politician of the mid-19th century. Leading light in the Anti-Corn Law movement, President of the Board of Trade, friend of Abraham Lincoln.

Anna Friel and Sue Devaney, top TV actresses.

Jack Howarth and Julie Goodyear Albert Tatlock and Bet Lynch of TV's *Coronation Street*.

Jack Howarth, Coronation Street's Albert Tatlock, born in Rochdale in 1896.